— THE **UNTOLD STORY** OF —
SARAH KEYS EVANS

CIVIL RIGHTS SOLDIER

BY DR. ARTIKA R. TYNER

CAPSTONE PRESS
a capstone imprint

Published by Capstone Press, an imprint of Capstone
1710 Roe Crest Drive, North Mankato, Minnesota 56003
capstonepub.com

Library of Congress Cataloging-in-Publication Data is available on the Library
of Congress website.

ISBN: 9781669004882 (hardcover)
ISBN: 9781669004837 (paperback)
ISBN: 9781669004844 (ebook PDF)

Summary: Most people have heard about Rosa Parks's brave actions that led to
the Montgomery Bus Boycott of 1955. But there were other Black women who
also challenged segregation in transportation. Three years earlier, Sarah Keys
Evans—a soldier—refused to give up her seat on a bus traveling through
the South.

Editorial Credits
Editor: Ericka Smith; Designer: Sarah Bennett; Media Researcher: Svetlana
Zhurkin; Production Specialist: Katy LaVigne

Image Credits
Alamy: Danvis Collection, cover, 4, IanDagnall Computing, 23; Associated
Press: 21, BHR, 26, File/Horace Cort, 15; Dreamstime: James Nesterwitz, 7;
Getty Images: Bettmann, 8, 25, 27, Don Cravens, 24, Frederic Lewis, 19; Library
of Congress: Prints and Photographs Division, 9, 17, Prints and Photographs
Division/Carnegie Survey of the Architecture of the South, 6, Prints and
Photographs Division/U.S. Farm Security Administration, 11; Newscom:
Everett Collection, 22; Shutterstock: Julia Khimich (background), cover (right)
and throughout, Nadegda Rozova (background), cover (left) and throughout;
Smithsonian Institution: National Portrait Gallery, 13; U.S. Army: 29;
Wikimedia: State Archives of North Carolina, 10, 12

TABLE OF CONTENTS

Words in **bold** are in the glossary.

STANDING UP FOR WHAT'S RIGHT

In the summer of 1952, Sarah Keys Evans took a bus ride that would change her life. A member of the Women's Army Corps (WAC), she wore her military uniform as she boarded a bus in New Jersey. She was headed to North Carolina to visit her family while on a break. She took a seat in the middle of the bus.

The bus arrived at Roanoke Rapids, North Carolina. A new driver took over. When he checked tickets, he demanded that Evans move to the back of the bus and give her seat to a white Marine. Evans refused. She was arrested and spent a night in jail. She also received a fine.

Evans later filed a **lawsuit**. Her three-year battle would become one of a series of little-known legal cases that would help end the practice of **segregating** passengers on transportation in the South.

Many people have heard of Rosa Parks and perhaps Claudette Colvin. Fewer have heard of Sarah Keys Evans. This is her story.

FACT During the Jim Crow era, many Southern states had laws that required segregating people by race in many public spaces. On buses, Black people were forced to give up their seats to white passengers and move to the back of the bus—where there might not be a seat available. The back of the bus was also hotter and filled with fumes from the engine when the windows were open.

CHAPTER 1

HARD WORK AND DETERMINATION

Evans was born Sarah Louise Keys in 1929. She was born in Washington, North Carolina. She had six siblings. Her parents, David and Vivian Keys, taught their children the importance of hard work and determination.

A courthouse in Evans's hometown of Washington, North Carolina

Evans went to nursing school in Perth Amboy, New Jersey.

Evans attended a segregated Catholic high school. She was known for being shy and quiet. After graduating from high school, she moved north. She attended nursing school in New Jersey.

In 1951, Evans joined the WAC. She could further her education and develop new job skills. She could also travel and meet new people.

Black Women in the WAC

In 1943, the U.S. Army created the WAC—previously the Women's Army Auxiliary Corps (WAAC). It gave women the chance to build careers in the military. Dr. Mary McLeod Bethune fought for Black women to have access to these opportunities. Being in the military provided Black women with education, training, and career choices. Some women also traveled overseas. Most Black women had limited job options during the Jim Crow era. Often they worked low-paying jobs as laborers and domestic workers.

Dr. Bethune with a new WAAC recruit in 1942

For Black people, serving in the military offered the possibility of being treated equally. Many believed they would no longer be treated as second-class citizens after their service. Unfortunately, they still faced discrimination—both during their service and after returning home.

WAC members arriving at Fort McClellan, Alabama, in 1954

With the hard work and determination her parents taught her, Evans completed her military training. She became a receptionist at a military hospital at Fort Dix in New Jersey.

CHAPTER 2

REFUSING TO MOVE

In August 1952, Evans was on her way home to spend time with her family. She had a long trip from New Jersey to North Carolina.

During a stop in Roanoke Rapids, North Carolina, a new driver took over and more people boarded the bus. The driver checked everyone's tickets. When he made it to Evans, who was seated in the middle of the bus, he demanded she give up her seat to a white Marine.

Evans knew her rights—that she didn't have to give up her seat. "I'm comfortable here," she replied.

The driver left the bus and returned a few minutes later. He told everyone else to leave the bus. He told Evans she could stay where she was but that the bus was not going anywhere that night.

The bus station in Roanoke Rapids

Private Bus Companies and Segregation

In 1946, the United States Supreme Court ruled in *Morgan v. Virginia* that segregation on buses traveling across states was illegal and struck down a Virginia law. States could not make laws that made interstate commerce—business between states—difficult. Seating passengers based on several states' laws would make interstate travel difficult.

This ruling made state laws that were discriminatory illegal—but not the discriminatory practices of private companies. So private bus companies—like Carolina Coach Company, which operated the bus Evans was on—continued to segregate passengers by creating their own rules.

A Carolina Coach Company bus in the 1940s

Evans tried to talk to the driver, but he wouldn't let her get on another bus. Then, she was arrested by two white police officers. When Evans asked why she had been arrested, she was told the charge was **disorderly conduct**. It was late and dark. She was afraid and worried about her safety.

Once Evans arrived at the police station, she asked to call her family. Evans was told she could not. The police officers told her that they would make the call for her. They never did.

Evans was taken to a cell. The bed had a filthy mattress, so she decided not to sit or sleep on it. She remained standing the whole night. Still in her uniform and high-heeled shoes, she paced the floor and prayed for her safety.

FACT Many Black women have challenged segregation on public transportation. In 1884, journalist and suffragist Ida B. Wells was forced off a train in Tennessee after she refused to leave a car designated for white passengers. She sued the railroad company and won, but that decision was later overturned by Tennessee's supreme court.

Ida B. Wells around 1893

The next day, Evans was brought to the chief of police. The chief asked what she was wearing. "You don't know the color of the United States Army uniform?" Evans responded. The chief threatened to slap her. He gave her a $25 fine, and she was put on a bus to Washington, North Carolina.

At first, Evans hadn't intended to fight the charges. But her father—a Navy veteran—challenged her to do so. Her decision to fight her unjust treatment would lead to a three-year court case. Her case would help end segregation in transportation.

A segregated trolley in Georgia in the 1950s

FIGHTING FOR JUSTICE

Evans's legal battle was not easy. First, she tried fighting the disorderly conduct charge. She lost. Then, the National Association for the Advancement of Colored People (NAACP) connected her with **attorney** Dovey Johnson Roundtree.

Roundtree helped her build a case against the practice of segregation. For Roundtree, the case was personal. She had also served in the U.S. Army. About a decade earlier, she'd had an experience similar to Evans's while in uniform.

Roundtree (right) with Dr. Bethune in the 1940s

FACT In 1943, Roundtree was a member of the WAAC. While she was in Miami recruiting soldiers for the U.S. Army, she sat in the front section of a bus. When Roundtree refused to give up her seat to a white man, the driver forced her off the bus.

Evans, Roundtree, and other lawyers on the case decided to build a federal case. They filed a complaint with the **Interstate Commerce Commission (ICC)**—*Sarah Keys v. Carolina Coach Company*. It would challenge the discrimination Evans faced by calling attention to a federal law on **interstate commerce**.

The Interstate Commerce Commission building in Washington, DC, in the 1940s

On November 7, 1955, the ICC ruled in favor of Evans. The ICC agreed that the segregation Evans experienced had been "undue and unreasonable prejudice and disadvantage," which violated the Interstate Commerce Act of 1887. This win meant that companies with buses that traveled between states could no longer segregate people.

This case helped chip away at segregation on transportation. A similar case ended the practice on railroads. Other cases struck down segregation in other spaces too, like bus stations. But many companies continued the illegal practice of segregation anyway.

A sign for a segregated waiting room at a train station in Mississippi in 1956

CHAPTER 4

PART OF A MOVEMENT

Although not well known, Evans's case was one of several efforts to challenge racial segregation during the mid-1900s. Ending segregation on transportation—across states, in town, in waiting rooms, on dining cars—was a huge battle.

Years before Evans's case, in 1947, activists had tested the ruling in *Morgan v. Virginia*. They organized a series of trips called the Journey of Reconciliation. Black and white activists took trips by bus from Washington, DC, through several states in the South. Some had no trouble.

Others were met with violence. And some were arrested. This showed that segregation on buses traveling between states was still being enforced.

Riders on the 1947 Journey of Reconciliation

On March 2, 1955, 15-year-old Claudette Colvin refused to give up her seat to a white woman on a bus in Montgomery, Alabama. Colvin was arrested. This angered Black residents of Montgomery. They organized to help support Colvin's case. Rosa Parks, the secretary of the local NAACP chapter, played a big role in that work.

Claudette Colvin

Nine months later, on December 1, 1955, Parks refused to give up her seat on a bus to a white man. She too was arrested.

Black residents of Montgomery once again went to work. They created the Montgomery Improvement Association (MIA), led by Dr. Martin Luther King Jr. The group organized a **boycott** of the local bus system. The Montgomery Bus Boycott lasted for 381 days. It ended after the Supreme Court ruled in a related case—*Browder v. Gayle*—that the city and the state could not segregate buses.

Black residents of Montgomery walking during the boycott instead of riding buses

Rosa Parks and the Montgomery Bus Boycott

Rosa Parks is known as the "mother of the Civil Rights Movement" because of her courageous action in December 1955. But she had a long history of activism in Alabama.

In the 1930s, Parks worked with her husband, Raymond, to help defend the Scottsboro Boys—a group of young Black men who had been falsely accused of a crime. She joined Montgomery's NAACP chapter in 1943. As a member, she traveled around the state documenting cases of discrimination and violence against Black people and helping them seek justice. She helped Black people register to vote. And, in 1949, she led the NAACP's youth council, which organized challenges to segregation.

Rosa Parks

By the time of Parks's arrest, she was a well-respected member of Montgomery's Black community. And Black community leaders had been working to end segregation for a while. With a well-known activist to support, an active community, skilled organizers, an engaging leader, and news coverage that brought them support from around the country, the Black community of Montgomery waged its biggest fight yet—and won.

Even after so many victories, racial segregation continued in public spaces, including on transportation. In 1961, the Freedom Riders—a group of Black and white people—decided to *again* test the ruling against segregation on interstate travel.

Five Freedom Riders planning their route

Freedom Riders sit next to their bus after it was bombed in Alabama.

The group boarded buses in Washington, DC. They planned to end their trip in New Orleans, Louisiana. Riders were beaten and arrested at a stop in South Carolina and at several stops in Alabama. One bus was bombed in Anniston, Alabama. The violence received a lot of media attention. Eventually, the federal government felt forced to do something. By November 1961, the ICC created new rules to finally enforce desegregation in interstate travel.

CHAPTER 5

HONORING A HISTORYMAKER

In 2020, some 68 years after her arrest, Evans finally received recognition for her role in shaping civil rights history. The city of Roanoke Rapids, North Carolina, declared August 1st Sarah Keys Evans Day. The city also named a plaza after Evans.

A local artist named Napoleon Hill created a mural in Evans's honor for the plaza. It shows key moments in Evans's leadership journey, from her arrest to her legal victory. It's titled *Closing the Circle*.

In 2022, the state also placed a historic marker at the bus station where Evans was arrested.

These are all tributes to a woman who acted boldly with the courage to help make equal rights a lived reality for all.

Sarah Keys Evans in 2014

GLOSSARY

attorney (uh-TUR-nee)—a lawyer

boycott (BOY-kot)—the act of refusing to buy or use a product or service to protest something wrong or unfair

commerce (KOM-uhrs)—the exchange of goods and services, often between states or countries

disorderly conduct (dis-OR-der-lee KON-duhkt)—a legal charge for behavior that is offensive or disturbing

interstate (in-tuhr-STAYT)—going between two or more states

Interstate Commerce Commission (in-tuhr-STAYT KOM-uhrs kuh-MISH-uhn)—a group created by the Interstate Commerce Act of 1887 that controls transportation between the states

lawsuit (LAW-soot)—a disagreement that is decided in a court

segregate (SEG-ruh-gate)—to keep people of different races apart in schools and other public places

READ MORE

Bailey, Diane. *Ida B. Wells*. New York: Aladdin, 2019.

Cline-Ransome, Lesa. *Claudette Colvin*. New York: Philomel, 2021.

Nathan, Amy. *Take a Seat—Make a Stand: A Hero in the Family*. Lincoln, NE: iUniverse, 2006.

INTERNET SITES

Civil Rights Teaching: Sarah Louise Keys
civilrightsteaching.org/desegregation/sarah-louise-keys

Civil Rights Teaching: Transportation Protests: 1841 to 1992
civilrightsteaching.org/desegregation/transportation-protests

Sarah K. Evans Inclusive Public Art Project: Interview of Sarah Keys Evans
sarahkevansproject.com/who-is-sarah-keys-evans

INDEX

ABOUT THE AUTHOR

Dr. Artika R. Tyner is a passionate educator, an award-winning author, a civil rights attorney, a sought-after speaker, and an advocate for justice. She lives in Saint Paul, Minnesota, and is the founder of the Planting People Growing Justice Leadership Institute.